Contents

Introduction

Social media marketing involves leveraging social platforms to engage both new and existing customers through a blend of entertaining, educational, and promotional content. Businesses utilize social media to promote products, enhance brand visibility, foster stronger customer connections, and significantly boost sales. This guide aims to introduce and streamline the essential aspects, enabling your organization to leverage the unique features of social media marketing for success.

Every week, major social media platforms like Facebook and X undergo significant changes, from algorithm updates to new advertising options on Instagram and Snapchat. We'll focus on leveraging social media marketing to achieve business goals. Starting with a social media audit, you'll learn to analyze findings, use data-driven insights, and tailor content marketing plans. Gain insights on refining your content mix, selecting the right social media platform, and crafting a comprehensive media strategy. Navigate the dynamic social media landscape confidently with a content marketing life jacket.

Effective social media copywriting is crucial for your brand's success, creating connections, motivation, and inspiring action. Crafting compelling content on platforms with fleeting attention is challenging. We'll discover tips, tricks, strategies, tools, and formulas to consistently produce memorable content your audience will love. Are you ready to unleash your creativity and become a social media copywriting master?

Being the one behind the publish button as a social media manager is a distinctive responsibility. This role is diverse, fulfilling, meticulous, and occasionally risky. Social media managers serve as the public voice of a brand, collaborate across the business, and employ various creative skills. However, challenges like burnout and the risk of sharing inappropriate information must be navigated. We'll focus on cultivating essential skills for effective social media management, addressing pitfalls, and providing guidance on succeeding in the role. A social media manager utilizes platforms such as TikTok, LinkedIn, and Twitch to enhance brand awareness, engagement, and conversions. As social media became a mainstream business tool, there are still limited guidelines, and we'll learn core competencies. Whether developing a strategy, creating content, managing a community, running ads, or measuring performance, we'll cover crucial aspects of a social media manager's responsibilities. Despite the ongoing anxiety, proper focus on skill development enhances confidence when hitting the publish button.

As a social media content creator for businesses, you juggle various responsibilities, including research, copywriting, and scheduling. The evolving nature of your role demands staying current. I'll share insights gained from helping businesses leverage social media for growth. We'll explore content creation basics, the step-by-step process, and valuable tools. You'll discover new tools and feel empowered as a social media expert.

The era of brief, impactful videos is here, benefiting not only Gen Z on TikTok but also offering a potent avenue for brands to connect with large audiences through platforms like TikTok and Instagram Reels. We'll explores contemporary marketing strategies, emphasizing the effectiveness of short-form videos in captivating and engaging viewers. From storytelling tactics to navigating algorithms and leveraging influencers, we'll explore what success looks like on TikTok and Instagram Reels. We'll learn strategies from brand strategists, social media marketers, influencers, and TikTok creators, which will provide valuable insights into the dynamic social media landscape.

We explore the power of social media stories, quick bursts of energy that capture your brand's essence. Learn how to develop a strategic approach, discover ideas aligned with your brand, and apply a simple storyboard technique. While platform-specific details aren't covered, master the tools on platforms like Instagram, TikTok, YouTube, Snapchat, or Pinterest separately. Make your brand's stories creatively stand out by integrating them into your content marketing plan and choosing the right platforms for your audience.

Chapter 1 Social Media Marketing

Produce an actionable social media strategy

A common mistake business makes when starting with social media is rushing into content creation without a well-thought-out strategy. Developing a social media strategy is crucial for setting goals, outlining specific steps, and organizing high-level themes and campaign details. The strategy varies in detail, with small businesses opting for concise plans and larger enterprises creating more extensive guides. The key is to ensure the strategy is actionable, guiding the development of effective social media campaigns. Define goals aligned with organizational priorities, identify target audiences through marketing personas, outline topics and content formats, choose the right channels, plan ongoing programs and short-term campaigns, and establish a publishing schedule. Thoughtfully planning your social media marketing strategy from the beginning avoids overeagerness and ensures a results-oriented approach.

Utilize this social media strategy template for organized, collaborative, and results-driven campaigns.

1. Set meaningful social media goals aligned with company objectives, defining goals and metrics.

2. Develop marketing personas by categorizing customers based on demographics and behaviors.

3. Create engaging content themes for organic and paid content on social media.

4. Choose the right social networks, defining primary and secondary purposes, content themes, and publishing frequency.

5. Organize social programs, campaigns, and tactics, estimating budget, resources, and staffing.

6. Establish a publishing schedule through an editorial calendar.

7. Build a social media marketing toolkit, incorporating tools for management, analytics, competitive intelligence, monitoring, research, visual production, and sourcing.

8. Stay updated on social media marketing trends through reputable sources like Adweek, Marketing Dive, Social Media Today, and Social Media Examiner.

Focus on social media measurement

Social media marketing offers no guarantees, but consistent measurement enhances the likelihood of success. Social media measurement involves setting relevant, achievable goals, tracking progress, and using performance data for decision-making. Meaningful goals are specific outcomes valuable to the business, achievable in a defined timeframe, and straightforward to measure. The three primary goal categories are conversions, engagement, and awareness. Conversion goals, such as sales and lead generation, are the most crucial. Engagement goals indicate interactions and feedback, while awareness goals focus on campaign visibility. Monitoring a mix of goals is ideal, choosing metrics aligned with specific goals and using established tools for calculation. A toolkit may include social network analytics and third-party tools. Generate regular reports to assess overall progress, campaign performance, and gather insights for future adjustments. Adapt based on feedback to improve social media effectiveness. Success in social media marketing is not guaranteed, but careful and continuous measurement enhances its likelihood.

Develop marketing personas for your audience

To avoid reaching no one on social media, create marketing personas to identify and target your audience effectively. Understanding demographics, challenges, and goals informs personalized messaging, crucial as 62% of consumers would abandon a brand for irrelevant experiences (Statista). Marketing personas are semi-fictitious profiles representing ideal customers, drawn from observations, analytics, CRM data, and formal research. Organize customers into groups, assign demographics and behaviors, and name each persona. Include relevant details such as age, job, education, location, traits, and interests. Highlight behaviors, challenges, and goals influencing purchasing decisions. For instance, the "Yogi Parents" persona might struggle with finding time for yoga. Identify communication preferences, listing preferred social media, influencers, podcasts, and publications. Use personas as a litmus test to ensure social media campaigns effectively reach your target audience.

To personalize social media messaging, define your audience based on demographics, challenges, and goals. Use the template below for creating marketing personas tailored to your organization:

PERSONA #1: NAME

Assign a name, and if relevant, include a title.

DEMOGRAPHICS

Include age, job title, location, education level, or other relevant attributes.

CHALLENGES: PAIN POINTS

Identify frustrations and barriers they are trying to overcome.

GOALS: MOTIVATIONS

Highlight what they are trying to achieve, both personally and professionally.

HOW OUR PRODUCT OR SERVICES PROVIDES VALUE

Describe how your organization uniquely addresses the needs of this customer group.

COMMUNICATION PREFERENCES

Identify specific online and offline sources of information they access.

Hire a social media manager

To maximize the potential of social media marketing for your organization, hiring a social media manager is crucial. The underestimated effort and expertise required for success often lead to lackluster results without proper support. A social media manager possesses the experience and skills to effectively manage platforms like Instagram, YouTube, and TikTok, building awareness, driving engagement, and improving conversions. Their focus on channels varies based on organizational type, size, complexity of marketing activities, and audience size. Regardless of channels, their consistent responsibilities include strategy, content creation, and community management.

In strategy, they contribute to defining and executing plans, ensuring ambition, modernity, and differentiation. Content creation involves developing engaging text, photos, videos, and more to fuel both proactive and reactive conversations. Proactive content initiates conversations on important topics aligned with goals, while reactive content responds to existing discussions. Community management involves ongoing efforts to maintain strong relationships with customers and partners, requiring consistent and personalized interactions to build trust and deliver business results. A social media manager is a critical hire for a lasting impact on these channels.

Community-based social networks

Instead of being active on every social network, carefully choose channels that align with your organization's goals. Impact and business value from a social network require a significant investment of time and resources, so it's crucial not to waste effort on the wrong platforms. Recognize the different types of social channels, such as community-based networks like Facebook, Instagram, X, and LinkedIn. These networks rely on users following accounts of friends, family, and colleagues, serving as platforms for public updates and community interaction.

Businesses benefit from advertising to engaged audiences with personalized content on these networks. Each channel has unique nuances and use cases. Facebook, a pioneer in mainstream social media, is effective for paid advertising campaigns. Instagram, also owned by Facebook, is visual and ideal for businesses selling visually appealing products. X, known for text-based Tweets, is in transition, and its role is uncertain. LinkedIn, a professional network owned by Microsoft, is trusted for recruiting talent and targeting business-minded customers, especially relevant for B2B organizations. Carefully consider these community-based networks when planning your social media mix.

Discovery-focused social platforms

Lean back and enjoy the discovery-focused social platforms—TikTok, YouTube, Twitch, and Pinterest—that entertain and inspire users with engaging content tailored to their interests. Unlike social networks focused on personal connections, these platforms are where users spend time discovering content for entertainment or learning purposes. While anyone can upload content, only a small percentage of the audience, usually creators and businesses, actively publishes. Users rely on advanced algorithms, search functionality, and following creators to discover quality content on these platforms. TikTok and YouTube, where users spend an average of 45 minutes per day, present opportunities for businesses to gain organic visibility and advertise to new audiences. TikTok disrupts social media with its superior algorithm, making it a leading platform for short-form videos.

Businesses benefit by collaborating with creators, advertising with user-generated content, creating original sounds, songs, and video series. YouTube, owned by Google, is a popular platform for watching various videos. Businesses can build connections through their own channels, providing in-depth content that reaches new audiences through searches on YouTube and Google. Advertisers can target audiences through ads before, during, or after popular videos. Twitch, a live streaming network owned by Amazon, focuses on live broadcasts, primarily of video game play with commentary. Businesses can reach younger audiences through ads or sponsor popular streamers on this niche platform. Pinterest, a visual search engine, is ideal for companies selling visual consumer-facing products. Businesses benefit from targeted ads and long-term conversions with search, as 85% of weekly Pinners make purchases based on brand Pins. Choose the platforms that align with your goals to pair messaging with the engaging experiences users expect.

Social Channel Selection Checklist:

1. Are your customers active on this social network?

2. Does this channel have a big enough audience to be worth an investment?

3. Do you have the resources to maintain an account on this channel?

4. Does your organization have the expertise to succeed here?

5. Are your competitors and industry peers active on this channel?

6. Is it possible to achieve your marketing goals on this platform?

7. Can your company afford to pay for advertising on this social network?

8. Can you reasonably measure and report results for this channel?

9. Have you personally tested this network to understand how it's used?

10. Does this channel facilitate customer service requests for your customers?

11. Are you able to experiment on this network, moving beyond best practices?

12. Will this social channel continue to exist in the long-term?

13. Are there creators active on this channel that you can partner with?

14. Is this channel brand safe and unlikely to threaten your reputation?

Social messaging apps

Social messaging apps, such as WeChat, Facebook Messenger, WhatsApp, and Snapchat, provide private communication channels where users can exchange messages individually or in small groups. Unlike traditional texting, these apps are free, globally accessible, and often offer enhanced mobile functionality, with some prioritizing security for private connections among friends and family. For businesses, these apps offer opportunities for customer service through manual responses or automated chatbots. Additionally, brands can run ads to engage with new and existing customers, encouraging interactions.

1. WeChat: A sophisticated Chinese messaging app functioning as an all-in-one platform for communication, bill payments, product purchases, and video chats. Ideal for businesses targeting consumers in China, it requires a strategic approach involving content publishing, advertising, collaborations with key opinion leaders, and the creation of mini programs.

2. Facebook Messenger and WhatsApp: Owned by Facebook, these private messaging services are commonly used for real-time customer service. Businesses leverage these platforms to address customer inquiries, provide canned responses to frequently asked questions, and utilize chatbots for automated experiences. Targeted advertising within users' inboxes and custom integrations, such as branded chatbots, are key features.

3. Snapchat: A pioneering social messaging app known for its concept of disappearing private messages. While primarily focused on ephemeral content, Snapchat allows brands to safely advertise in select publishers' public stories. Companies can also feature short video ads between creators' stories and create branded lenses and filters. Notably, customer service interactions are limited on Snapchat due to the temporary nature of shared content.

As online conversations increasingly shift to private channels, businesses should consider these messaging-based social networks to stay connected with their active audiences.

Review sites and discussion forums

Consumers prioritize recommendations over advertisements, turning to review sites and discussion forums for informed decision-making. Review sites, such as Yelp, TripAdvisor, G2, Google Business Profile, OpenTable, Amazon, and Facebook, serve as platforms where users can post reviews about products and businesses. These reviews are valuable for businesses to collect feedback, enhance offerings, and build trust among customers. To maximize impact, businesses should identify relevant review destinations, complete comprehensive profiles, encourage customer reviews, and thoughtfully respond to both positive and negative feedback.

Discussion forums, including Reddit, Quora, and Stack Overflow, allow users to ask and answer questions anonymously, fostering honest and raw conversations. Brands benefit from advertising on these forums, leveraging the opportunity to engage with a less ad-saturated audience and build authenticity.

By strategically utilizing review sites and advertising on discussion forums, businesses can cultivate trust with customers and effectively reach their target audience.

Create organic content for social media

Social media offers a unique opportunity to quickly share messages, primarily through organic content, which is free but may not guarantee visibility. Focus on creating engaging, relevant, and complementary content by identifying three to five overarching themes. For instance, a bedsheet and pillow brand might cover funny sleep commentary, giveaways, retail updates, philanthropy, and sleep-related how-to. Align themes with your marketing personas, addressing challenges and goals. Ensure the topics are logically connected to your brand. Develop an editorial calendar to thoughtfully plan and organize your messaging across platforms, maintaining a balance and maximizing efficiency. This strategic approach enhances customer connection and optimizes the impact of your organic social media content.

Produce engaging paid social campaigns

Paid social advertising, or paid social, allows you to target specific audiences at scale on social media channels. These ads, resembling organic posts, enhance visibility without seeming disruptive. Structuring a successful campaign involves defining goals (awareness, engagement, or conversions), specifying target audiences, creating compelling ads aligned with each platform's guidelines, setting a flexible budget, and monitoring and adapting based on performance. Paid social is effective at any business stage, providing immediate visibility and results, making it a valuable marketing tool to explore.

Humanize your content

In contrast to traditional marketing, social media thrives on authenticity. It's not about portraying a flawless brand but showcasing real, unfiltered moments. Whether through organic or paid social content, customers appreciate raw footage, behind-the-scenes challenges, business processes, beliefs, and the people behind the brand. Humanizing your content involves aligning with values and consistently communicating them. Examples include Ben & Jerry's addressing social issues or using self-deprecating humor or employee features. It's about commitment to values, not a one-size-fits-all formula. Start by showcasing your team, involving customers, and ensuring accessibility, making your brand more relatable and distinctive.

Embrace social listening and monitoring

Listening is vital in social media conversations, offering a unique platform for public interactions. Companies can gain valuable feedback, provide customer service, and join crucial discussions. Before engaging, businesses should embrace social media monitoring, tracking brand-specific conversations, and invest in social media listening, analyzing broader industry and trending topics. Monitoring focuses on addressing brand-related feedback, adapting to input, and managing reputation. On the other hand, listening involves understanding industry perceptions, analyzing competitors, and staying culturally relevant. While most companies prioritize monitoring for customer connection, not all commit to robust listening programs due to resource constraints. Utilize tools like Sprout Social or Hootsuite for monitoring, setting keyword alerts. For listening, rely on third-party enterprise tools such as Meltwater, Brandwatch, or Sprinklr to analyze industry-wide conversations efficiently. Timely and accurate reporting is crucial for both monitoring and listening efforts, providing insights for informed responses and staying relevant in social media conversations.

Proactive engagement to earn attention

Initiating conversations on social media is a powerful strategy for gaining positive attention. Proactive engagement involves starting or contributing to discussions that provide real-time value and showcase your expertise, anticipating your customers' needs. This approach aims to foster meaningful interactions, educate, and entertain your audience. For instance, TurboTax might use Instagram to discuss financial literacy for teens, showcasing expertise beyond tax services. Social listening guides proactive engagement, allowing your brand to join relevant conversations and strengthen its reputation. It's essential to lead discussions on topics that offer tangible value, position your brand as a leader, and align with your values. To ensure success, actions must align with social media messaging, fostering trust and encouraging participation in discussions. When deciding to join existing conversations or comment on trends, assess relevance, potential value addition, and appropriateness for your brand. Utilize social media for proactive engagement, shaping conversations positively and enhancing your brand's image.

Reactive engagement for customer service

Responding to customer inquiries, expressing gratitude, and resolving issues on social media enhances customer loyalty and builds a positive reputation. This form of engagement, known as reactive engagement, involves addressing direct outreach from customers, be it for support or feedback. The goal is to retain customers by consistently responding to their queries and resolving issues promptly. For example, Spotify utilizes its Spotify Cares X account to publicly acknowledge and address user concerns, often guiding them to private messages for specific issue resolution, ensuring privacy and limiting negative exposure. To implement reactive engagement, use social monitoring to track messages across platforms like Facebook, TikTok, Instagram, etc. Respond promptly, acknowledging and ideally resolving queries or complaints with conversational, professional, and concise communication. Always maintain a public acknowledgment, demonstrating active responsiveness. Respond within 24 hours, balancing speed with quality and personalized care. Additionally, recognize and appreciate non-service-related comments, feedback, or reviews to strengthen brand loyalty. Deliver exceptional customer care on social media through meaningful responses that swiftly address customer needs.

Customer Service on Social Media

Adopting effective social-first customer service involves key steps:

1. Identify Relevant Channels:

   - Determine platforms where audience feedback is received.

   - Examples: Facebook, X, Instagram, Google Business Profile, Yelp, etc.

2. Monitor Feedback:

   - Assess the volume of mentions and business locations.

   - Decide between manual monitoring, free tools, or paid solutions.

3. Choose Tools:

   - Select monitoring and reputation management tools based on needs.

   - Examples: Keyhole, Moz Local, Talkwalker, ReviewTrackers, etc.

4. Respond to Feedback:

   - Prioritize responses: negative feedback, customer queries, positive reviews.

- Craft effective responses: friendly greeting, acknowledgment, apology, resolution, gather information, explain action, move to private forum.

5. Timely Responses:

  - Respond promptly, preferably within 24 hours, focusing on issue resolution.

6. Private Forum Transition:

  - Shift negative discussions to private messaging while acknowledging publicly.

7. Pattern Recognition:

  - Create a spreadsheet to log service requests and identify trends.

  - Use insights to prevent issues and enhance resources like tutorials and FAQs.

Coordinate teams with a social media policy

In social media marketing, success is a collaborative effort, akin to a symphony needing an entire orchestra. While led by the social media manager, effective activities involve coordination with various teams. Internal partnerships should support key initiatives and secure necessary resources. Establishing a social media policy guides collaboration, outlining rules for all company activities on social media. This document, not to be over-engineered, empowers the team with streamlined requirements. Regular communication with other departments ensures awareness of activities, identifies opportunities for social media support, and promotes tighter coordination. Understanding the goals of partnering teams helps set expectations and ensures impactful collaboration. Celebrate progress to showcase the value of contributions and elevate social media as a coordinated effort within the company.

Social Media Team's Cross-Departmental Support

1. C-suite Executives:

  - Train executives for thought leadership.

  - Build personal brands through social media.

2. Marketing:

  - Coordinate social media across campaigns and mediums.

  - Showcase company culture and employee stories.

- Gain insights for FAQs and customer experience improvement.

- Source topic inspiration from customer feedback.

3. Sales:

  - Utilize LinkedIn and B2B channels for prospect research.

  - Personalize outreach through social media.

4. C-Suite/Internal Communications/PR:

  - Pitch engaging social media content for additional media coverage.

  - Develop and enforce a social media policy.

  - Train employees on public discussions about the company.

5. Human Resources:

  - Use social media to attract job applicants.

  - Distribute company news internally through social channels.

Set up successful creator campaigns

In the current landscape, consumers rely more on creators than brands, with 37% trusting a creator's opinion over a brand's statement about a product. Creators, also known as influencers, play a crucial role in the sales cycle on social media due to their earned trust and massive followings. Creators, who engage consistently with their audience on various platforms, are effective at persuading their followers to take action, making them valuable partners for businesses seeking to break through the social media noise. Companies can collaborate with creators in various ways, such as sponsoring posts, sending free products for reviews, or even co-creating products for mutual benefit. The key is to align with creators who resonate with your target audience and share relevant topics, ensuring a genuine partnership that earns the trust of their followers.

Creator Selection Checklist

- Topic Relevance: Does the creator discuss topics related to your organization, ensuring alignment with your brand?

- Audience Reach: Does the creator have a sufficiently large audience, meeting your organization's outreach goals?

- Audience Engagement: Is the creator's audience actively engaged with their content, indicating a meaningful impact?

- Audience Alignment: Does the creator's audience match your ideal customer profile, ensuring relevance?

- Brand Safety: Does the creator's content align with your brand's guidelines on key topics, ensuring brand safety?

- Channel Choice: Is the creator active on channels frequented by your audience, optimizing visibility?

- Content Format: Does the creator use content formats preferred by your audience, enhancing resonance?

- Partnership Costs: Does your organization have the budget and resources for creator partnerships, meeting compensation expectations?

Questions to Ask

- Topic Relevance: Has the creator discussed topics related to your organization, such as personal hygiene for a toothpaste brand?

- Audience Reach: Does the creator reach a large enough audience, meeting your organization's criteria for collaboration?

- Audience Engagement: Is the creator's audience actively engaging with their content, with satisfactory views and comments?

- Audience Alignment: Does the creator's audience match your ideal customer profile, ensuring relevance?

- Brand Safety: Does the creator's content align with your brand's guidelines on key topics, ensuring a safe partnership?

- Channel Choice: Is the creator active on channels preferred by your audience, ensuring optimal visibility?

- Content Format: Does the creator use content formats preferred by your audience, enhancing resonance?

- Partnership Costs: Does your organization have the budget and resources for creator partnerships, meeting compensation expectations?

Experiment beyond best practices in social

Relying solely on best practices won't yield significant results in social media. Constantly experimenting and evolving your approach is crucial for exceptional outcomes. Once mastering best practices, creatively bend or ignore them to enhance your brand through experimentation. This may involve early adoption of new social media features, unconventional collaborations with creators, or championing social causes. For instance, HP, a tech company, garnered 5 million TikTok views with an unexpected sustainability campaign, showcasing their cartridge recycling program through TikTok creators. This experiment succeeded by being distinctive, engaging, and aligning with customer interests, associating HP with environmental preservation.

To conduct successful social media experiments:

1. Choose a Singular Focus: Direct efforts on promoting a single product, utilizing a specific feature, or trying a particular tactic.

2. Define Goals: Establish clear goals benchmarked against past results, such as increased media mentions, to gauge experiment success.

3. Set a Timeline: Ensure a defined start and end date for the test, allowing sufficient time for resonance, often within a campaign or over a month.

4. Monitor Progress: Track real-time progress, adapting strategies based on what resonates with the audience.

5. Document Results: Record outcomes to avoid duplicating efforts, facilitate learning, and inform future experiments.

Innovating on social media requires experimentation beyond conventional best practices.

Stay updated on social media marketing

Feel empowered to engage in purposeful social media marketing. Prepare to craft your strategy, guiding your team towards customer impact and business value. To excel continually, stay informed about emerging channels, marketing advancements, and evolving approaches. Subscribe to news sources like "Social

Media Today," "Social Media Examiner," "Adweek," and "Marketing Dive" for up-to-date insights. Success in social media isn't guaranteed, but strategic decision-making significantly enhances the likelihood of positive outcomes.

Chapter 2 Social Media Strategy and Optimization

How to build your social media strategy

Describe your company's social media approach as strategic, targeted, and customer-centric, with a focus on continuous testing and adaptation. Emphasize integration throughout the organization, recognizing that social media is a permanent and dynamic aspect of the business landscape. Stress the importance of managing social media programs in harmony with overall plans, maintaining brand character and voice across platforms. Highlight the need to tailor content to each channel, understanding when to adjust the corporate tone. Shift from traditional marketing to editorial thinking, prioritizing customer relationships, and delivering valuable content. Value and measure social media efforts in alignment with business goals, emphasizing quality over quantity. Recognize the evolution from early days of content volume to today's emphasis on strategic, creative, and excellent content. Avoid being seen as a content polluter and remember that selling requires a nuanced approach beyond repetitive messaging.

How to identify and segment your customers

Understand your customers and their belief in your brand by delving into customer insights. Start with audience segmentation, utilizing demographics such as income, education, age, and job to target messages effectively. Psychographic targeting goes beyond demographics, considering customer values, emotions, and attitudes. Collect information with permission and adhere to regulations to protect customer privacy. Behavioral data, including responses to calls-to-action and repeat orders, paints a comprehensive picture. Analyze demographics, psychographics, and behavior to tailor social media content to customer preferences. Pay attention to engaging content, social media platforms, and conduct social listening to identify customer activity and competitive opportunities. Ultimately, knowing your customers' perceptions and preferences is crucial for creating content that meets their wants and needs.

How to conduct a social media audit

Many organizations adopt a platform-first approach to digital media, leading to multiple accounts, abandoned profiles, and an ineffective content plan. To address this, companies should conduct a social media audit, examining strengths, challenges, and media effectiveness. The audit should encompass internal and external factors, including competitor analysis, customer conversations, and stakeholder input. It is crucial to set goals and objectives for the audit, maintain objectivity, and scrutinize various digital assets for improvements. A well-executed social media audit provides insights for developing a strategic roadmap aligned with social media goals.

To conduct an effective social media audit, organizations should move beyond a platform-first approach and assess their current state, including multiple accounts, lacking policies, and unclear goals. Start by listening to customer, competitor, and stakeholder conversations. Develop a SWOT analysis to understand strengths, weaknesses, opportunities, and threats. Analyze results, identify trends, and gain insights. Tailor the audit with questions about target audience, platform usage, competitor actions, strengths, weaknesses, and internal barriers. Establish goals, review website and social media properties, and interview internal and external stakeholders. Conduct an environmental scan of competitors and analyze findings for a strategic plan with actionable recommendations. Customization is key to addressing organizational needs.

How to analyze your SWOT and adapt your social media plan

In today's complex world, big picture thinking remains essential in SWOT analysis. Strengths and weaknesses focus inward, while opportunities and threats look outward. Honesty is crucial in assessing your position, avoiding a lengthy list and keeping it concise, tying observations to business goals. Using Cake Design as an example, strengths include community recognition, creativity, and name recognition. Weaknesses include high expectations, managerial issues, staff turnover, and inconsistent social media posting. Opportunities include an online recipe subscription and becoming a baking expert for a show. Threats include a former employee starting a competing business and potential competition from a national bakery chain. Evaluating these factors suggests Cake Design should position Amanda as an influencer, hire a manager, and invest in social media strategy for sustained success.

Social media platforms and their superpowers

Navigating social media can be overwhelming due to constant changes and platform overlap. It's crucial for businesses to identify platforms that facilitate meaningful connections with their customers. Major platforms from Facebook, including Facebook, Instagram, and WhatsApp, cater to diverse audiences, with Instagram appealing more to a younger demographic. YouTube excels in social video, TikTok redefined video entertainment, Snapchat utilizes video effectively and leads in augmented reality. X is a newsfeed platform, LinkedIn offers diverse content beyond business networking, Pinterest focuses on aspirational content and social shopping. Other platforms like Tumblr, Reddit, Discord, and Clubhouse cater to specific communities. Tailor your brand's approach based on research, social listening, and strategic considerations aligned with your customers, brand, and resources.

How to boost awareness with ads and promoted posts

Viral organic posts from brands are no longer effective; paid opportunities on social media platforms have taken their place for monetization. To incorporate paid media into your social media plans, consider options such as boosting or promoting posts, video or photo ads, pre-roll and mid-roll ads, carousel ads, brand takeovers, and sponsoring hashtags or trending topics. Custom assets like augmented reality lenses can be created through collaboration with platforms. Tailor your paid and organic post blend based on your business goals, whether it's building awareness, sparking consideration, or encouraging purchases. Define your budget, target audience, campaign length, geography, and content type. Platforms offer AI or algorithmic optimization for automated updates, but regular monitoring and adjustment are essential for effectiveness.

Social commerce meets the four Ps

For bricks-and-mortar retailers or those venturing into online stores, social commerce is a valuable strategy for connecting with customers and providing convenient product access. Apply a digital twist to the four Ps of marketing—product, price, place, and promotion. Focus on visually showcasing products in photos and videos, considering different views and AR try-before-you-buy options. Determine pricing strategy, factoring in costs, profit margins, customer willingness to pay, competitor pricing, and additional costs like shipping and returns. Ensure a secure and user-friendly checkout and payment system. Choose social media platforms strategically, treating your main site as a flagship and social integrations as stores. For promotion, employ a mix of paid, earned, owned, and shared media, managing content and engaging with customers effectively. In social commerce, prioritize the "people" aspect, aiming for memorable, shareable, and enjoyable interactions that meet customer expectations.

Influencer marketing and the creator economy

Marketing and the creator economy are flourishing as influencers and creators attract followings based on their passions. Choosing the right influencers for your brand can be challenging. For those with substantial budgets, digital or traditional stars may be an option, but building closer relationships is possible with micro-influencers (under 10,000 followers) or even nano-influencers (1,000 to 5,000 followers), who often drive high engagement due to their close connection with followers. In the creator economy, influencers make money through various platforms' creator funds, tips from viewers, and direct brand partnerships. Platforms like Facebook, LinkedIn, TikTok, Pinterest, and Snapchat offer creator funds, while others like YouTube, X, and Clubhouse allow tipping. Brands can collaborate with influencers through live stream shopping events, social commerce, brand events, product launches, and sponsorships in podcasts, newsletters, or video content. Transparent disclosure is crucial for maintaining audience trust. To start, establish your budget, decide between reach or niche, define success metrics tied to business goals, set expectations, and build long-term relationships with influencers aligned with your brand values. Allow influencers the freedom to create within the agreed scope.

How to create stories

Once upon a time, a little yellow ghost, known as Snapchat, invented the Stories format—a popular feature now adopted by Instagram and Facebook. Stories are brief, episodic narratives combining various elements like images, video, text, filters, emojis, gifs, doodles, polls, and hashtags. Ideal for capturing events, announcements, or a day-in-the-life of your brand, Stories usually vanish in 24 hours, allowing for real-time, low-production-value content. To create an engaging Story, start with a clear idea or framework, considering the emotions you want to convey and your call to action. The episodic format benefits from a focus or plot, and testing different visuals is key. Develop a rough storyboard to visualize scenes, keeping a vertical layout for easy viewing on mobile phones. Prepare a script in advance, considering short bursts of descriptive text for emotion, but allow for adaptability and spontaneity. Mix up the visuals to avoid a monotonous look. Stories provide quick bursts of creativity, offering an authentic glimpse into your brand's personality.

Harness the immediacy: Livestream video

Not long ago, video production was costly for companies, but with the rise of social video and Facebook's introduction of livestreaming, the landscape changed. X, YouTube, TikTok, and LinkedIn soon followed suit. Livestream video allows brands to connect directly with their audience, offering immediacy and authenticity. To create compelling livestreams, engage in pre-production work for watchable and entertaining content. Possible content includes product launches, behind-the-scenes interviews, talk shows with guests or internal panelists, and collaborations with influencers. Tailor content to your audience and platform. Livestream video is versatile, serving as a tool for customer service, crisis communication, and more. To start, establish goals, define your concept, format, and target audience, choose channels, and acquire basic equipment. Develop a workflow covering pre-production, promotion, going live, and editing. Conduct a pilot before going live, promote on social channels, gather audience feedback, and adapt accordingly. When livestreaming, give it your all and go with the flow.

How to build connections with podcasts and social audio

Podcasts have gained popularity due to their flexibility, allowing listeners to engage anywhere. They're cost-effective and offer creative storytelling possibilities. Whether targeting customers or an internal team, a podcast must address audience needs. Choose a format, determine equipment needs, establish a workflow, and plan promotion. Social audio, resembling podcasting, is more immediate and interactive. Platforms like X or Clubhouse facilitate real-time discussions with hosts, presenters, and listener participation. Be prepared for candid feedback, as social audio encourages open dialogue. Whether opting for podcasting or social audio, start with a compelling idea, involve the audience, and anticipate their reactions for a successful conversation.

Gaze into the future: Marketing in the metaverse

The metaverse is a buzzword, but its full realization is still in progress. Current virtual worlds like Facebook's Horizon Worlds, Decentraland, Roblox, and Second Life offer a glimpse. The metaverse's future may include both virtual and augmented reality, requiring marketers to stay informed on both fronts.

Immersive marketing possibilities are vast, such as creating virtual scenes for brands. However, challenges like disclosure of paid interactions, user privacy, and interoperability standards need addressing. Marketers must be creative, considering sci-fi for inspiration, reimagining customer interactions, and collaborating with tech partners to navigate this evolving landscape and create meaningful digital connections with customers.

How to refine your brand's social media content mix

Navigating the evolving landscape of content marketing requires a focus on customer resonance. Understand your audience by analyzing demographics, behaviors, and relationship data. Tailor your content to meet their needs and preferences, considering platforms and content types that align with your brand. Prioritize relationship-building over constant sales messages. Optimize your content strategy by viewing it as a series, not isolated posts. When choosing a content management platform, assess factors like budget, team size, and existing partnerships. Experiment with platforms to find the best fit. Ultimately, successful content marketing centers around understanding and aiding your customers, fostering meaningful relationships at every step.

How to optimize paid, earned, shared, and owned media

Social media, once a platform for personal connections, evolved into a business model with the introduction of advertising and promoted posts. The PESO model (Paid, Earned, Shared, Owned) emerged, emphasizing the integration of various media disciplines. Facebook, initially for organic content, now accommodates a mix of PESO media. Your challenge is to find the right combination for impactful customer engagement. Prioritize customers and content over media buys. Embrace the 3Ps—publish, produce, promote—while choosing a PESO mix aligned with your budget, objectives, and data-driven insights. Adopt a scientific mindset to test, analyze, and optimize content across social and traditional media for budget efficiency and goal achievement.

Measure what matters to your brand

Once you've outlined your audience, devised a plan, and chosen social media channels, the next step is measuring your brand's impact. Utilize a marketing funnel to track awareness, interest, desire, and action. Social media platforms often offer analytics dashboards, and website analytics tools like Google Analytics can provide additional insights. Analyze data using descriptive analytics (e.g., visits, bounce rate), predictive analytics (based on historical data), and prescriptive analytics (identify patterns and potential corrective actions). Track search and keyword ranking, use trackable links for influencers, monitor Marketing Qualified Leads (MQLs) and Sales Qualified Leads (SQLs) aligned with your CRM system. Establish actionable metrics, set benchmarks, and adapt as needed to achieve your business outcomes.

Continue your social media strategy journey

Not long ago, brands questioned the relevance of social media, but now the focus is on strategic adaptation for improved customer engagement and Return on Investment (ROI). We recommended starting with a social media audit, providing a comprehensive guide to assess platforms, analyze data, and create customer-centric stories. Exploring top social networks, content creation, refining the content mix, selecting the right management platform, and optimizing plans based on audience needs are essential strategies for staying ahead in the dynamic landscape of social media. The only certainty is continuous change, but a compelling story remains a consistent key to captivating customers.

Social Media Plan Template Overview:

- Describes the intended achievements and immediate barriers.

- Example: One-paragraph description for launching a blog, specifying its type, target audience, post frequency, etc.

Goal(s):

- Clearly outlines what you aim to achieve.

Strategic Considerations:

- Points addressing challenges, issues, and opportunities, often including competitive landscape analysis.

- May be presented as a SWOT analysis.

Objectives:

- Quantifiable, SMART objectives tied to evaluation.

- Example: Increase blog readership by 20% by December 31.

Audience:

- Identifies target audience, possibly segmented with demographic and psychographic data.

Strategy:

- Describes how overall goals and objectives will be achieved.

Tactics:

- Actionable steps to bring the project to life, involving blog posts, social media updates, contests, videos, ads, etc.

- Integration with traditional marketing channels.

Budget:

- Includes out-of-pocket expenses, agency costs, and staff time.

Timeline/Responsibilities:

- Shows how elements align to achieve objectives, includes responsible parties.

- Clearly states timing and duration of critical decision points.

Results:

- Evaluation based on measurable objectives, summarizing achievements and shortcomings.

Learnings/Recommendations:

- Post-program assessment noting success, areas for improvement, changes, and actionable recommendations for the future.

Chapter 3 Copywriting for Social Media

Creating a buyer persona for social media

According to author and entrepreneur Seth Godin, you may not be able to change everything or everyone, but you can impact the people who matter for your business. To identify these crucial individuals, start by creating a buyer persona for your social media posts. This persona, a detailed representation of your target audience, includes demographics, interests, goals, challenges, and behaviors. Begin by analyzing current customer data, consulting customer service or sales teams, and conducting surveys or interviews. Collect information such as location, age, interests, challenges, and values. For B2B businesses, consider industry, business size, and job title. Identify the challenges your audience faces, understand their goals, and tailor your strategy to help them overcome obstacles. This process allows you to craft copywriting that resonates directly with your audience.

Establishing your brand's voice

As a California-born surfer, imagine launching a custom wetsuit shop targeting millennial surfers in Hawaii and the US West Coast. Your initial social media post, however, lacks the expected casual, enthusiastic, and fun tone that matches the brand image. Beyond identifying your audience, it's crucial to consider how you communicate with them—the essence of your brand's voice. Your brand voice is your personality, influencing how you stand out and connect in a crowded space. Define your mission, values, and desired feelings for your customers. Determine what role your brand plays (coach, friend, mentor) and specify what it shouldn't sound like. Incorporate this voice consistently across social media, ensuring your team aligns with it. Ready to build a brand voice that resonates? It's about staying true to yourself.

Review copywriting tips

Mastering social media copywriting is more science than art. To convert passive followers into fans, understand each platform's purpose; what works on one may fail on another due to community and etiquette differences. Overcome reader objections, such as time, money, self-doubt, trust, or complacency, by addressing missing information in your content. Lastly, make it personal. Speak directly to the reader, utilizing the buyer persona you've crafted. Effective copy is conversational and reader-focused, minimizing the use of brand-centric terms. With these basics, you're equipped to craft inspiring social media copywriting.

Understand copywriting formulas

Mastering copywriting starts with a quick and easy way to consistently create compelling copy. Effective copywriting formulas, such as the four Ps (Promise, Picture, Proof, Push) and PAS (Problem, Agitation, Solution), have been successful for decades. The four Ps involve making a promise, painting a vivid picture, providing proof, and giving a push to take action. For instance, as a pillow manufacturer, you promise a peaceful slumber, paint a picture of waking up refreshed, offer proof through customer surveys, and push for orders. PAS tackles problems, agitates them, and presents solutions. For on-call IT support, state the problem of remote work challenges, agitate them, and provide the solution of 24/7 IT support. Choose the formula that fits your business best, and watch your content become more magnetic and memorable.

Write copy for Facebook

On Facebook, with its billions of users, brands have a massive opportunity to connect with potential customers. To stand out, personalize your content by knowing your audience through buyer personas. Engage your audience with open-ended, conversational questions. Starbucks asks about favorite drinks, showcasing their customization options, while Target triggers positive nostalgia by asking about favorite teenage accessories. Adapt your language to match your audience; Glossier uses emojis for a youthful vibe, while Tough Mudder employs fitness slang for exercise enthusiasts. Facebook is an ideal platform to experiment with creative copywriting and create engaging, likable posts for your brand.

Write copy for X

Did you know that more than 500 million tweets are posted daily? X offers a significant opportunity for brands, but standing out can be challenging due to the character limit of 280. To master copywriting on X, focus on concise formatting. Avoid cluttered tweets with excessive hashtags and unclear calls to action. Choose a cleaner layout with a couple of relevant hashtags and provide context for links. Trigger emotions by creating curiosity or incorporating humor, making your content memorable and shareable. Add visuals to enhance your message, ensuring they complement rather than distract from your copywriting. Explore top brands on X for inspiration and consider applying these practices to elevate your brand.

Write copy for Instagram

Instagram, known for visuals, offers vast potential for brands. Crafting impactful captions adds context to images and videos, making your brand's message memorable. Ensure voice consistency, whether witty or storytelling. Hook readers with a compelling first line as only the initial 125 characters are visible.

Use sensory words to engage different senses—sight, sound, touch, taste, and smell—for a more immersive experience. Apply these tactics to transform your Instagram captions from ignorable to unforgettable, boosting overall engagement and brand success.

Write copy for LinkedIn

For professionals on LinkedIn, engaging content can still be creative. Enhance your posts by focusing on self-development, emphasizing benefits over features, and mastering effective calls to action. Understand that LinkedIn users seek growth and career development. Incorporate terms like growth, success, leader, mistakes, habits, productivity, and goals. Prioritize simplicity in language and make content easy to consume in short breaks. The key is a compelling call to action that guides users on the next steps. Craft engaging posts, fostering conversation or prompting action, and unlock the potential for creativity on LinkedIn.

Readability apps for social media posts

To enhance your social media copywriting, prioritize readability. Use tools like Hemingway App, which analyzes reading comprehension levels, word count, and suggests simplifications. Another option is the Readability Analyzer, which calculates readability scores and highlights difficult words. If you want to assess existing content, try Juicy Studio's readability test by pasting the post URL. These tools ensure your copy is clear and digestible, providing valuable content that resonates with your audience.

Spelling and grammar tools

Prioritize spelling and grammar to maintain professionalism on social media. Tools like Expresso and Grammarly help analyze and correct text, addressing weak verbs, filler words, and sentence structure issues. With Expresso, paste your text, analyze it, and click on each metric to correct highlighted words. Grammarly, available as a desktop app or browser extension, underlines errors as you type, providing suggestions for corrections. Utilize these tools to enhance your writing and prevent mistakes, establishing a polished image for your brand.

Use headline analyzers for social media posts

Capture your audience's attention immediately on social media by focusing on the first sentence, especially on platforms like LinkedIn, where only a snippet is visible. Use headline analyzers like Sharethrough's and the Advanced Marketing Institute's to enhance your copywriting. Sharethrough's tool evaluates emotional appeal and suggests improvements, while the Advanced Marketing Institute's tool calculates emotional value and identifies the targeted brain area. Elevate your social media content by considering these tools to make your opening lines more compelling and engaging.

Use thesaurus and dictionary apps for social media copy

Choose your words wisely when crafting copy, as they can evoke various emotions. Access convenient and creative tools to enhance your vocabulary. WordHippo is a versatile and free tool that provides synonyms, antonyms, definitions, rhymes, sentences, and pronunciation for any word. For visual learners, Visuwords visual thesaurus generates an interactive map with color-coded synonyms, antonyms, and associated words for your chosen word. OneLook's reverse dictionary is perfect for finding words based on a concept or definition, helping you articulate ideas when the exact word eludes you. Explore these online tools to elevate your vocabulary and impress your audience.

A/B testing social media copy

Despite having a powerful copywriting formula and inspiring examples, social media marketing remains challenging due to its dependence on audience reactions. However, there's a strategy to boost your chances of eliciting a positive response: A/B testing your social media content. A/B testing involves comparing two versions to determine which resonates better with your target audience. Consider elements such as emoji usage, post length, tone, text formatting, calls to action, and hashtags for testing. Focus on a specific goal for each post, such as converting readers to website traffic or attracting new audience members. Decide whether to test on your entire audience or a segmented portion. Ensure minimal variations between versions to pinpoint the impact of the tested element. For instance, if you run a bakery targeting engaged couples, you might test different calls to action about wedding cake flavors. Experimenting with content through A/B testing allows you to understand your audience's preferences and refine your copywriting accordingly. It's not just about creating content but also about experimenting and refining based on results. Embrace the role of a content scientist and start testing your social media content.

Leverage audience feedback in posts

Creating social media copy can feel like speaking into the digital abyss. To avoid mistakes, seek audience feedback through methods like social listening, polls for product/service ideas, asking open-ended questions, and actively reading comments. Spending time in the comment section helps understand your audience's challenges and preferences, providing a competitive edge in crafting valuable content.

Review analytics for social media post-performance

To enhance your social media copywriting, prioritize analyzing performance through platform-specific analytics. On Facebook, access insights by clicking "see more insights" under the manage page dashboard. For Twitter, click on "analytics" in the menu. On Instagram, check insights for the last 7, 14, or 30 days, including follower growth and activity patterns. LinkedIn offers a snapshot on your page and detailed analytics via the "analytics" dropdown. Leverage this wealth of information on each platform to inform and improve your copywriting strategies.

Continue refining your social media copywriting skills

Armed with the essential tips and tools, you're equipped to foster reader relationships and craft a compelling brand narrative online. However, true mastery in copywriting requires an ongoing commitment to learning. Dive into new formulas, explore strategies, delve into the psychology of influence, and practice consistently to discover what resonates.

Chapter 4 Essential Skills for Social Media Managers

Create a social media strategy

Social media managers can draw valuable strategic insights from journalism practices. In journalism, a compelling story addresses key questions: who, what, when, where, why, and how. Similarly, a robust social media strategy should thoughtfully answer these questions, outlining how the organization will leverage social media for business outcomes. A social media strategy is a documented plan that guides social media activities, helping prioritize time and resources. Regardless of an organization's size or industry, developing a strategy is crucial for informed decision-making in social media investments. It enhances a social media manager's leadership skill, improving the chances of success. This strategic document showcases contributions to the company, ensuring consistency as collaborators contribute to social media efforts. Whether a small business with a concise strategy or a large brand with an in-depth one, the general elements and structure remain similar. Utilize the fundamental questions journalists address as the six sections within your social media strategy:

1. Why: Define the purpose of using social media, specifying goals and metrics for measurement, focusing on conversion, engagement, and awareness.

2. Who: Identify the target audience on social media, creating customer personas based on geographic, demographic, behavioral, and psychographic traits.

3. What: Determine the topics and content formats to connect with customers and achieve goals, focusing on subjects relevant to customers and related to the business.

4. Where: Decide on social media platforms to be active, considering impact and effectiveness rather than being on every platform.

5. When: Establish a publishing schedule for consistent updates and reactions to content, recognizing the rapid nature and short shelf life of social media.

6. How: Bring the strategy to life by outlining programs, campaigns, and tactics, specifying ongoing initiatives, activities with end dates, and important actions for results.

Recognize that this document is an evolving resource requiring regular updates, akin to a journalist refining a well-rounded story. Use this framework to create a comprehensive strategy for a results-oriented approach to social media.

Plan with an editorial calendar

An editorial calendar serves as a crucial guide for social media managers, offering detailed direction for day-to-day messaging. It goes beyond scheduling posts and ensures diverse, relevant campaigns across various channels and formats. The value lies in sharing a variety of content to address different customer needs, maintaining engagement, and experimenting with resonant themes. For instance, Patagonia utilizes Instagram, Twitter, and Facebook to cover environmental topics through essays, photos, and documentaries, catering to diverse customer preferences. The editorial calendar should balance proactive and reactive content. Proactive content, the majority, is planned messaging around set themes to educate or entertain customers, offering unique insights. Reactive content responds to customer feedback, industry news, or relevant discussions, providing a timely perspective to build trust and awareness. Create your own editorial calendar to direct details and ensure your social media activities align with your goals.

Research your industry and pop culture

A significant challenge for social media managers is staying ahead of industry trends, competitors, and the latest social media updates. Consistent research is essential to maintain an informed perspective for timely responses and trend awareness. To simplify the process, regularly refer to credible sources such as podcasts, newsletters, social media accounts, webinars, and insights from colleagues. Organize these sources into three categories: Industry insights, current events, and social media trends. Industry insights focus on sector-specific updates, competitor analysis, and shifting customer needs. Current events cover cultural moments impacting messaging. Social media trends help adapt strategies to new features and opportunities. Utilize reliable sources like industry publications and trending sections on social networks for comprehensive research. This approach ensures you're well-equipped to guide your organization's social media activities.

Polish your writing skills

Effective social media content creation involves writing, whether for video scripts, image captions, or posts. Given the fast-paced nature and character limits of platforms like X, concise writing is crucial. Establish a consistent voice for your brand, reflecting traits like humor, inspiration, or authority. Mirror your audience's voice for relatability, but avoid forced attempts. Use plain language for easy understanding, avoiding jargon. Clearly define your post's goal, whether to entertain, educate, or persuade. Incorporate hashtags judiciously for content discovery, and use emojis to express brand personality. Include a clear next step in posts to guide reader action. These writing fundamentals enhance your social media presence.

Prioritize your design skills for social media

Design serves as the bridge between information and comprehension, as stated by artist Hans Hofmann. In the context of social media, well-designed visuals, combined with effective copy, enhance content performance. Purposeful decisions in design contribute to brand memorability and initial attention in the newsfeed. When capturing images, consider composition by identifying the subject, using the rule of thirds, and ensuring clarity, especially on small screens. For graphic design, establish a style guide for consistent colors and fonts, prioritize simplicity to convey the main message, and use design tools like Canva for ease. Implementing these strategies ensures that design becomes an asset rather than a hindrance in conveying your message on social media.

Grasp filming and recording foundations

Audio and video content excel on social media, offering richer storytelling opportunities compared to text and images alone. As a social media manager, developing skills in filming videos and recording audio enhances your versatility. Follow these six steps when creating content: choose a valuable topic, capture attention in the first few seconds, consider the platform's orientation, add captions for accessibility, select an engaging thumbnail, and repurpose content for wider distribution across multiple networks. These steps increase your chances of success in creating compelling social media content.

Host as on-camera talent

As social media becomes a more authentic space, social media managers are increasingly taking on the role of on-camera talent for their company's accounts. This shift is aimed at humanizing brands and fostering connections with audiences. To successfully host brand social media, managers should engage in more content creation, become product experts, and develop a conversational on-camera presence. This involves becoming proficient in recording and editing content, gaining in-depth knowledge of products, and practicing confident and comfortable on-screen delivery. Regular practice and experimentation will enhance these skills, making social media managers effective on-screen hosts for their organizations.

Rely on content curation

Content curation is a powerful tool for social media managers, saving time and expanding content. It involves finding and presenting information from various sources, adding personal insights. Strive for an 80-20 balance, with 80% being original content and 20% curated. Curate content responsibly by crediting sources and offering unique perspectives. Use different curation types, such as aggregation, synthesizing, and remixing, to provide diverse and engaging content. Content curation is an essential and efficient approach for social media success.

Monitor and respond to customer feedback

Social media offers a unique platform to cultivate a community, often overlooked by businesses focused on one-way messages. Community management, crucial for social media managers, involves consistent interaction, feedback response, and showcasing user-generated content. Social listening helps find relevant conversations, allowing engagement without direct promotion. Actively seeking feedback through AMAs, live events, or Q&A sessions fosters collaboration. Lastly, spotlighting community members and their content builds a supportive environment, contributing to an authentic brand narrative. Successful community management on social media involves engaging, collaborating, and highlighting user contributions.

Provide customer service on social media

Social customer care, a facet of community management, involves resolving customer issues on platforms like X and WhatsApp. While larger companies often have specialized teams, smaller businesses rely on social media managers. Essential principles of customer service apply: respond promptly, empathize, apologize when needed, and resolve issues efficiently. Three unique guidelines for social customer care include the expectation for quicker responses, addressing complaints publicly initially, and ensuring a seamless transition if moving to another service channel. Delivering exceptional customer service on social media involves timely, authentic, and considerate interactions.

Distinguish paid advertising and organic promotion

Using social media for businesses is not entirely free. While it may have lower costs compared to other marketing channels, it still demands a budget, resources, and skills. Social media involves both organic and paid aspects, each with distinct costs and benefits. Organic social media entails sharing content that might be seen by followers, with costs associated with content creation. It relies on audience engagement and algorithms for visibility. In contrast, paid social media involves advertising, guaranteeing exposure through targeted campaigns. It requires a budget for immediate results. Successful social media managers often use a combination of organic and paid strategies to balance costs and drive results effectively. Integrating top-performing organic content into paid ads can be a cost-effective approach. While not entirely free, social media provides various options that offer significant value to businesses.

How to manage paid social campaigns

A successful paid social campaign involves three phases: plan, personalize, and publish. Start by setting campaign goals, focusing on conversions for optimal results. Determine the budget needed and adjust based on campaign priorities. Personalize the campaign by targeting specific audiences and tailoring ad creative and copy to their needs. Experiment with various ad elements to optimize effectiveness. Finally, monitor ad performance closely, reallocating budgets to successful ads and discontinuing underperforming ones. Successful social advertising requires thoughtful planning, personalization, and ongoing optimization.

Partner with stakeholders internally

A social media manager plays a coordinating role within an organization, collaborating with various stakeholders and teams. Collaboration involves partnering with internal teams, such as customer service or PR, to fulfill job requirements. Building relationships with colleagues is crucial, regardless of organizational size or individual independence. To foster collaboration, regularly communicate and seek feedback, ensuring alignment with organizational goals. Socialize campaigns by updating relevant coworkers, highlight progress through impactful reporting, and advocate for colleagues by proactively offering support. These actions position the social media manager as a reliable and supportive partner within the organization.

Collaborate with external partners

One effective way to grow your social media audience is through partnerships with creators and companies that share similar followers. By collaborating, both parties can reach a broader customer base with shared interests. As a social media manager, you can identify and manage potential partnerships. There are two types of partnerships: low touch (informal interactions, e.g., commenting on content) and high touch (formal, paid engagements with shared goals). Finding partners involves assessing brand safety and researching their recent activities. Once partners are selected, manage expectations through meetings and creative briefs, ensuring effective communication and alignment of goals.

Social media managers play a crucial role in identifying, researching, and managing collaborations with external partners for audience growth.

Analyze social media goals and metrics

Measuring social media effectiveness can be confusing, with questions about the significance of followers versus engagement or the uniformity of video views on different platforms. To gain clarity, establish business-focused goals and relevant metrics. Goals represent key business outcomes, such as a 10% increase in brand engagement. Metrics, like mentions and comments, help gauge progress toward these goals. Create a measurement scorecard with a concise list of two to four goals and two to three metrics per goal to maintain focus and ensure a holistic view of progress. Prioritize conversion goals for key actions, followed by engagement and awareness goals. Choose a mix of goals from all three categories to guide diverse social media activities. This approach minimizes confusion, providing a clear understanding of social media impact and its integral role in your marketing strategy.

Use a mix of measurement tools

Many social media marketers fall into the trap of solely focusing on surface-level metrics like likes and views, as they are quick and familiar. To avoid this, measure the comprehensive impact of your social media activities across conversion, engagement, and awareness goals. Use a variety of measurement tools to save time and enhance accuracy. Analytics dashboards in social media management tools such as Hootsuite and Sprout Social provide a centralized view of activities across multiple platforms. Web analytics tools like Google Analytics help understand website traffic from social media, aiding in analyzing campaign effectiveness. Reputation management tools, or social media monitoring tools, track brand mentions across various sources, helping manage customer sentiment and identify potential crises promptly. Invest in a robust toolkit to ensure your measurement efforts are both comprehensive and focused on essential insights.

How social media managers evolve

The role of a social media manager is dynamic, bringing both joy and stress due to its constant evolution. Embrace the excitement of learning new customer engagement approaches while acknowledging the challenge of staying updated. Allocate weekly time for both passive learning (such as courses, podcasts, articles) and active learning (hands-on experimentation) to enhance your skills and adapt to shifts in social media. As the landscape evolves, consider specializing in specific channels and disciplines to navigate the growing complexity.

Chapter 5 Content Creation Strategy and Tools

Why strategic content creation matters

Content is crucial in today's digital age, where consumers are online, and traditional marketing methods are outdated. Strategic content creation, estimated to reach 4,000 to 10,000 daily exposures, is vital for standing out in the crowded digital landscape. The first benefit is audience growth and trust building. Consistent delivery of valuable content fosters relationships and builds trust with your ideal audience. Another advantage is establishing authority in your industry by regularly creating inspiring, educational, and entertaining content. Lastly, strategic content creation contributes to lead generation. Each shared content piece increases the potential for new traction and generates leads when sparking interest. Effective social media content, embraced by 80% of marketers, is a crucial part of digital marketing plans, making content creation an essential technique for business growth. Get excited about strategically creating content on social media to propel your business forward.

Outlining the content creation process

Content creation can be perceived as either fun and easy or time-consuming and frustrating. To establish a robust process, follow the four phases of ideation, planning, creation, and scheduling. In the ideation phase, generate ideas guided by research, considering audience interests, common questions, struggles, objections, and mistakes. Researching competitors can also provide insights. In the planning phase, use a content calendar to organize ideas, sort them into pillars, choose platforms, and set publication times. This phase ensures purpose and direction for each piece of content. The creation phase involves making content, which can be intimidating for those without prior experience. User-friendly tools and content batching, where multiple pieces are created in advance, enhance efficiency. Finally, in the scheduling phase, use a scheduling tool to automate posts, allowing for publishing on multiple platforms at specified times. This process optimizes efficiency, freeing up time for other brand-related tasks.

Using Ubersuggest to research topics and generate content ideas

Social media platforms, such as Instagram and LinkedIn, use algorithms to organize content on users' feeds based on relevance rather than chronology. Creating engaging content that stands out amid social media competition can be challenging and time-consuming. Ubersuggest, an online keyword research tool, simplifies the process by generating relevant content ideas for your target audience. By entering industry-related keywords, Ubersuggest provides an overview of keyword popularity and suggests related keywords. The tool also offers a content ideas report, showcasing popular blog posts based on the searched keywords. Ubersuggest's power lies in providing a vast array of ideas and allowing you to analyze both successful and underperforming content. However, it's crucial to avoid replicating content and instead use insights to understand audience preferences. Repurposing ideas into various content formats, such as static image posts, carousel posts, articles, or TikTok videos, enhances versatility and engagement. Ubersuggest streamlines the ideation phase, offering valuable insights into search trends, helping you produce focused and compelling content for your target audience efficiently.

Using Airtable to plan and organize content

Creating content involves multiple steps and can be overwhelming. Keeping track of posting schedules, content organization, and team communication can be challenging. A content calendar proves invaluable in addressing these challenges for your social media strategy. Despite the initial commitment, it ensures long-term payoff, reducing stress, ensuring consistency, and promoting strategic planning. Unlike tools like Google Calendar and Google Spreadsheets, Airtable stands out due to its user-friendly interface and customization options. The Airtable content calendar structure includes fields for scheduling, content ideas, attachments, captions, style planning, and post status. It facilitates collaboration by allowing easy sharing with team members and clients. Customization options enable tailoring to fit unique team processes. Creating different views provides flexibility in visualizing data. While the provided template is one way to structure an Airtable content calendar, customization options allow users to adapt it to their specific needs. Understanding the significance of a content calendar and how to structure it with Airtable's template empowers users to create their personalized content calendars.

Using Wordtune to write compelling and impactful copy

Copywriting is a crucial aspect of content creation, but if writing isn't your strength, you might worry about engaging your audience effectively. However, there's a solution – meet Wordtune, a versatile tool functioning as your copywriter, editor, and style guide. Powered by AI, Wordtune analyzes your copy for grammar, errors, and clarity, making it an essential tool for content writers. It offers two usage options: an editor page or a Chrome extension. With the extension, simply install it, and Wordtune will appear in writing environments like Google Docs. You can fine-tune sentences by highlighting and using the rewrite feature, providing multiple suggestions for improvement. The free version offers the rewrite feature, while the premium version introduces formal/casual rewrite options, shorten/expand features, and a word finder for non-native English writers. Wordtune saves time, making the editing process quicker and ensuring error-free, high-quality content creation. Give it a try to enhance your writing experience and boost your confidence in producing impactful copies.

Using Canva to design captivating social media graphics

As a social media content creator, effective visual communication is essential. The visual aspect of your posts can capture your audience's attention and encourage further engagement. Canva, a popular graphic design platform, is used to create compelling social media designs. Whether you choose a free or pro account, navigate to the social media button, where you'll find various formats for popular platforms. You can start with a blank post or explore Canva's template library for inspiration. Templates are customizable, allowing you to edit elements like titles, colors, and backgrounds to align with your brand. Canva's template grids make image replacement easy. Access the extensive design library, search for specific elements, and drag them into your design. Canva's intelligence search helps find images with specific characteristics, streamlining the design process.

Using Mojo to create engaging video content

Video content is an enduring and impactful tool, with studies revealing that brands using videos enjoy 31% more traffic. To enhance your video creation, consider utilizing Mojo. While initially marketed for Instagram stories, Mojo is versatile, supporting animated video creation for various platforms like LinkedIn, YouTube, and Pinterest. It offers beautifully designed and easily customizable templates for different business types. Mojo's free version includes a decent template selection, while Mojo Pro (premium) provides more templates and animation effects. To get started with Mojo, follow these steps: choose a template, customize it using various options like color, music, format, duration, and text. After editing, preview and export the video. Mojo allows direct sharing to Instagram stories or saving the video for other platforms. All designs are stored in Mojo for easy access and modifications. Create engaging and professional video content effortlessly with Mojo, suitable for various platforms such as Instagram stories, LinkedIn posts, or Pinterest video pins.

Using Facebook Creator Studio to automate posting

Once your detailed content plan is ready and content creation is complete, efficiently schedule and manage your posts using Facebook Creator Studio. This integrated tool serves as a centralized hub for social media marketers, offering content management, monetization, and tracking for Facebook and Instagram accounts. To utilize Creator Studio, go to business.facebook.com/CreatorStudio or access it from your personal page menu. Click the "Create Post" button to initiate scheduling for Facebook, selecting the desired page if you manage multiple ones. For Instagram, choose the Instagram icon in Creator Studio and proceed similarly. Customize your posts with captions, media, and distribution options, then either publish immediately or set a specific date and time. For Instagram, the scheduler currently works for feed posts and IGTV. Additionally, explore other features within Creator Studio, including Insights for performance metrics, the Inbox for managing interactions, and the Monetization tab for exploring ad opportunities. Mastering Creator Studio allows you to focus on content quality while efficiently managing your social media presence.

Chapter 6 TikTok and Instagram Reels Marketing Strategy

Modern digital marketing strategies

On platforms like TikTok and Instagram Reels, brands can employ modern marketing strategies, specifically focusing on brand marketing and content marketing. Brand marketing goes beyond logo exposure, encompassing a brand's identity, uniqueness, personal story, and promises to customers. Effective storytelling in brand marketing builds a positive brand impression, fostering customer preference. Content marketing, on the other hand, involves creating valuable content to attract and retain an audience, aiming for customer engagement and action. It emphasizes providing what the audience wants, without a hard sell, and often works well on social media platforms. While brand marketing pushes content to the audience, content marketing pulls them in by offering relevant content. The unique dynamics of short-form video platforms make them ideal for both approaches, as audiences appreciate transparency and enjoy engaging content that aligns with brand identity and values. These platforms organically serve content, emphasizing the significance of content marketing in building brand loyalty.

The role of short-form video in social media marketing

Short-form video is an ideal medium for both brand and content marketing, fostering authenticity that builds trust and customer loyalty, crucial as 90% of consumers value authenticity in brand preference. Different social media platforms have distinct strategies for short-form video regarding length, format, style, and target audience. While shorter videos are generally favored due to an average eight-second attention span, brands find success in repurposing content across platforms. A strategic approach involves crafting a central theme or idea and repurposing it for various platforms, enhancing reach and impact. Considering the marketing funnel, short-form videos on TikTok and Instagram Reels excel at capturing awareness, generating interest, and fostering consideration throughout the funnel. The TikTok algorithm's personalized For You feed introduces users to new brands and products, making it effective top-of-funnel content. Educational content, behind-the-scenes, FAQs, and tutorials work well for top-of-funnel engagement. As users move down the funnel, brands can create content showcasing deals, promotions, product reviews, interviews, and more. Calls to action, whether direct or subtle, can lead to conversions. The key is to create personal, relevant, and thoughtful videos with a hook, story, and emotion, aiming for more views, higher engagement, and increased customer acquisition.

Techniques to create strong short-form video

When creating short-form video content, immerse yourself in the platform, observe competitors, analyze viral videos, and identify gaps to fill. Start publishing without waiting for perfection to receive feedback and learn what works. Crafting a compelling 15-second narrative takes practice, and condensing it to five sentences is effective. Use strong hooks within the first three seconds, considering the fast-paced nature of platforms like TikTok and Instagram Reels.

Engage viewers with closeup faces, movement, and compelling graphics. Include clear, relevant on-screen text and be human, connecting authentically with your audience. Anticipate your audience's needs, research keywords, and create diverse content types to capture wider audiences. By following these principles, you'll consistently produce engaging short-form videos.

Digging deeper: TikTok

TikTok stands out in the social media landscape due to its full-screen, full-sound, immersive auto-play videos, fostering high user engagement. Beyond dance trends, TikTok features diverse content like DIY tutorials, brand stories, and behind-the-scenes videos. Its algorithm provides a level playing field, allowing anyone to go viral. This discovery platform, with a personalized "For You" page, enables brands to organically reach target demographics. TikTok's democratizing tools simplify content creation, making everyone a potential creator. Despite its Gen Z focus, TikTok's audience spans all ages, emphasizing the importance of authenticity. TikTokers seek connection, encouraging brands to showcase their human side. Short, engaging videos thrive on TikTok, where audience engagement is notably high. For brands aligning with TikTok's audience, it offers a great opportunity for strategic marketing initiatives.

Digging deeper: Instagram Reels

Instagram Reels emerges as a major competitor, introduced in 2019 to capitalize on the trend of immersive short-form video. Like TikTok, Reels offers full-screen, full-sound, immersive auto-play videos, integrated with Instagram filters and editing tools. Reels is seamlessly incorporated into the platform, appearing in Instagram Stories and the explore feed. Just as TikTok's For You page customizes content, Reels aims for personalized content, aligning well with target demographics. Authenticity is crucial for success on Reels, showcasing a brand's human side. Content options include brand stories, product videos, mini-vlogs, user-generated content, how-to videos, and more. Reels provides a comfortable entry point for brands with an existing Instagram presence, offering higher engagement than main feed videos. For those exploring short-form video, especially on Instagram, Reels can amplify brand reach as part of a comprehensive social media strategy.

Top strategies for creating effective TikToks

To create compelling short-form videos on TikTok, focus on storytelling, authenticity, and engaging your audience with entertaining, educational, or inspirational content. Practice making 15-second videos to hone your storytelling skills and use tools like text overlays or voice-to-text for effective narratives. Blend storytelling with educational tips to create memorable and entertaining content. Consider featuring a recognizable face for your brand to enhance audience connection. Experiment with behind-the-scenes footage, fun filters, and licensed music, crucial to TikTok's social fabric. Leverage structural techniques like seamless loops and editing on cues. Interact with other brands to tap into TikTok's traffic-directing features. Consistency is key, with the best-performing brands posting three to four times per week. Cross-post strategically, but avoid duplicating content extensively to maintain authenticity and audience engagement. Keep your focus on delivering unique and audience-centered content for success on TikTok.

Understanding the TikTok algorithm

The TikTok algorithm and how you can use it to boost your brand. TikTok's algorithm operates by gradually circulating videos to more users if they receive high engagement from a small initial group. The "For You" page, TikTok's main page, is not based on accounts you follow but offers personalized content according to your preferences and engagement history. Unlike platforms like Facebook or YouTube, TikTok serves content to a relatively passive yet engaged audience, potentially leading to increased exposure without ad spending. Optimizing your content for the algorithm involves focusing on video engagement, completion rate, and strategic use of features like duet and stitch.

Short, engaging videos with a strong hook at the beginning tend to perform well. Additionally, labeling your video with relevant hashtags, trending sounds, and compelling captions helps the algorithm understand your content. Experimenting with hashtag strategies is crucial. Other factors, such as user information and language preferences, contribute to the algorithm's decision-making process. Adjusting certain aspects of your video based on performance data is a strategic approach. Consistent posting enhances your chances of reaching a broader audience through the "For You" page, leading to increased followers and brand visibility. Understanding TikTok's recommendation system sets the stage for creating videos that align with the platform's unique algorithm.

Using hashtags effectively

On TikTok, hashtags play a crucial role in categorizing and making your videos searchable. They inform the TikTok algorithm about your content, aiding in reaching the right audience. By effectively using hashtags, you can also identify competitors, industry connections, and expand your reach for more followers. Hashtags help segment content, providing users with categorized videos. While TikTok users rely less on searching, hashtags still hold value as users click on them to discover related content. The Discover page organizes popular videos based on trending hashtags. Using trending hashtags in your posts can enhance visibility and attract more views. Hashtags also contribute to the algorithm by indicating the video's content, complemented by a concise caption. Research industry-related hashtags to position your content effectively.

Creating a unique branded hashtag fosters community engagement and can lead to viral success. Ensure your hashtags are clear, relevant, and easily searchable, combining niche, global, and trending ones. Explore the Discover page for trending hashtag ideas and check popularity using the search bar or third-party tools like Hashtag Expert. Conduct hashtag tests with similar videos to refine your strategy. Avoid using high-traffic hashtags unrelated to your content, as this may negatively impact your brand and result in content hiding. Save your hashtag space for keywords relevant to your content rather than using #FYP or #Foryoupage, which has limited impact on landing on the For You Page.

Capitalizing on trends and challenges

Trends and challenges are distinctive features on TikTok, representing ever-changing cultural movements. Trends encompass a variety of activities, such as dances, skits, or videos using specific filters or effects, shared by thousands in unique ways. Challenges are a subset, involving users responding to a call to action with a challenge hashtag. The TikTok algorithm favors trends and challenges on the For You page, offering increased exposure. These elements foster a strong sense of community, connecting users who engage in mass collaborative efforts. Brands participating in trends enhance authenticity and connection with the audience, creating a fully developed brand personality.

While being part of popular trends is beneficial, brands should ensure alignment with their identity and not solely rely on trends for content. Successful trend participation involves being early, taking creative risks, and reducing bureaucracy for timely content. Creativity and personalization distinguish brand contributions to trends. While trends are valuable, brands should strategically use them sparingly to build trust and facilitate easier conversion into customers. Trends are integral to TikTok's dynamic culture, providing opportunities for brands to engage followers and spark community interest.

Leveraging influencers

TikTok influencers, successful creators with mass followings, offer a valuable strategy for brands to create strategic content, increase reach, and attract new customers. Influencers act as modern celebrity endorsements, establishing deeper connections through personalized, authentic engagement. Choosing the right influencers, those aligned with brand values and goals, is crucial for effective collaboration. Before partnering, brands should research potential influencers, assessing their authenticity, creativity, and trustworthiness across various platforms. Influencers should be approached with clarity on strategy, objectives, and deliverables, while allowing them creative control. Authenticity is key in influencer collaborations, ensuring content doesn't feel overly sponsored. Budgeting smartly for influencers involves considering factors like follower count and exposure. Collaboration with micro-influencers can be strategic, creating a trend for broader reach. Regardless of the approach, a strong alignment between creators and brands is vital for achieving successful results.

Creating ads

Brands can expand their TikTok presence through paid media integration, leveraging TikTok Ads to automate content creation and delivery. Adherence to TikTok's style guidelines is crucial, aiming for authenticity and a native feel. The five types of TikTok Ads include In-Feed Ads, Brand Takeover, TopView, Branded Hashtag Challenge, and Branded Effects. Each serves different purposes, with Branded Hashtag Challenges allowing brands to dictate campaigns. Disclosure of promotional content is essential, with options like #Ad or a branded content toggle. Initiating TikTok Ads is straightforward, involving registration and approval on the TikTok Ad signup page. Use organic content first for testing before converting successful videos into paid Ads. Embracing the unique TikTok advertising journey involves creating authentic content that seamlessly integrates with the platform's style.

Using other TikTok tools and techniques

In addition to leveraging the TikTok platform for brand growth, consider various tactics to enhance your TikTok strategy. Engage with your audience through comments, creating community and showing genuine interest. Utilize TikTok's unique comment features, allowing text or video replies for increased interactivity. Explore the duet and stitch features to foster collaboration within your niche and build a sense of companionship. Embrace user-generated content, seizing opportunities when TikTokers engage with your brand. Stay attuned to trending sounds and consider creating your own to potentially initiate a trend. Experiment with these engagement tools to discover what aligns best with your brand strategy.

Connections between Reels and TikTok strategies

Authenticity and style from TikToks work well on Reels too. However, Reels tends to have a more polished and produced feel compared to TikTok's raw spontaneity. Filters and idealistic content perform better on Reels. When comparing the platforms, TikTok has more advanced built-in editing features, while Reels' trends often rely on its built-in effects. Reels uses audio from TikTok, creating a unique relationship between the platforms. If transitioning from TikTok to Reels, consider editing options to avoid algorithm limitations. Uploading identical content to multiple platforms is generally discouraged, as it may be repetitive for viewers. Understanding what works on TikTok can benefit Reels content creation, as there's a high correlation between viral content on both platforms.

Understanding the unique selling points of Instagram Reels

Instagram Reels provides an excellent platform for brand engagement, especially if your target audience is already on Instagram. Utilizing short, engaging videos tailored to educate, entertain, and inspire can convert Instagram followers into loyal customers. If you have a substantial Instagram presence, incorporating Reels into your content strategy is advantageous, as Instagram's algorithm rewards creators using all in-app features. Reels offers a polished aesthetic, making it suitable for brands with a more refined style. Planning videos with defined goals, storytelling, and clear calls to action is crucial. Instagram's broader ecosystem enhances the reach of Reels content, appearing not only in the Reels tab but also in the Explore page, Instagram Stories, and even on Facebook feeds. Leveraging Reels requires adhering to social media best practices, addressing audience needs, providing educational and inspiring content, engaging with trends, and collaborating within your niche. Embrace the space and experiment to discover what resonates best with your audience.

Implementing your social strategy for TikTok and Reels

This is a thrilling moment for brands entering the short-form video realm, with TikTok and Instagram Reels attracting highly engaged audiences. Aligning your brand with these platforms' demographics, interests, and values, and committing to producing authentic, valuable content can yield a significant return on investment. Explore TikTok's Creator Portal and TikTok for Business resources for in-depth information and step-by-step directions. Before creating content, immerse yourself in the platform, analyze competitor strategies, explore potential collaborations, and embrace the world of shareable, authentic content. Enjoy the creative journey on TikTok and Instagram Reels, celebrating your brand's uniqueness to foster genuine connections with your target audience.

Chapter 7 Social Media Creative Strategies and Tips

Developing your story strategy for marketing success

Social media stories are brief visual narratives capturing moments, events, announcements, or daily activities creatively. Despite their easy creation and sharing, it's crucial to develop a strategy for your brand's stories to ensure creativity, consistency, and goal alignment. Consider where stories fit in your marketing plan, frequency of production, content development responsibility, streamlined approvals, budget allocation, and relevant KPIs for measurement. Assess competitors' stories, gather customer preferences, and seek inspiration from creators. Tailor your stories to your brand voice, ensuring they align with your brand image, whether aiming for luxury.

Generating story ideas for your brand

Social media stories are bite-sized glimpses of your brand, akin to content snacks. To connect with your audience, consider your company's personality—whether it's heroic, caring, humorous, or innovative. Express this in stories through informative or entertaining content, polls, moments, event promotions, or problem-solving. Keep stories simple and clear to prevent confusion. Draw ideas from existing media assets, identify high-performing content, and showcase memorable moments, cultural aspects, product launches, or behind-the-scenes interactions. Turn your stories into small gifts that enhance customer bonds. For example, a bakery business could share quick baking tips, Friday surprises, or amusing cooking mishaps to humanize the brand and foster relatability. Make stories enjoyable, creative, and diverse to maintain excitement and engagement from your audience.

Applying storyboard techniques to social media stories

Creating engaging social media stories often requires a thoughtful approach. Start with a simple storyboard, applying the rule of three to structure your story into a beginning, middle, and end. Whether digital or sketched on paper, this basic framework provides a foundation for pacing and direction. While not restricted to only three visuals, having clear starting and ending points ensures a cohesive flow. For example, a brand like H Plus Sports might chronicle a sponsored team's crucial game, starting with an empty stadium, transitioning to the team playing, capturing crowd reactions, and concluding with the team's celebration. The storyboard serves as a starting point, and your creativity comes into play as you incorporate various elements like video, photos, text, emojis, GIFs, and filters. Stay flexible and be prepared to seize spontaneous moments to enhance your stories.

Creating stories: From budget to production

Contrary to common belief, social media stories are not entirely free, despite their quick and easy production. Similar to earned media, a budget, team, and process are essential to ensure your compelling story doesn't go unnoticed. Begin by creating a simple budget, considering equipment, expenses, ads, sponsorships, and a contingency for unforeseen opportunities. Your team, likely within your content marketing group, should consist of individuals familiar with the stories format and open to creative experimentation aligned with your brand values. Look for visual storytellers with improvisational skills and a good sense of humor. Given the fast-paced nature of social media stories, streamline your workflow by adjusting the approvals process to allow flexibility for on-the-fly production. While maintaining quality standards, trust your team to create engaging stories. Additionally, develop a crisis plan for handling mistakes if they occur.

Enhancing stories with AR, stickers, and GIFs

Social media stories offer creators the opportunity to both show and tell, allowing for the incorporation of GIFs, doodles, emojis, music, and augmented reality filters. The key to a successful story lies in finding the right balance that aligns with your brand's personality. Avoid overwhelming your audience with excessive decorations, as the fast-paced format and limited screen space necessitate a "less is more" approach. Think of it like baking a cake – blend the right ingredients (emoji, AR, doodles, text) in moderation to surprise your audience, and customize them to match your brand. Just like a bakery business creating a mouthwatering cupcake, aim for a result that is neither too cluttered nor too subtle but just right for your brand.

Marketing and measuring social media stories in real time

Producing social media stories doesn't guarantee visibility, so define your goals and align your stories with them. Whether you aim to attract customers, promote products, drive website traffic, or provide entertainment, use marketing strategies. Encourage team members to share company stories, tag relevant people, use appropriate hashtags, and keep calls to action simple. Leverage other social platforms to talk about your stories, cross-post, or collaborate with influencers. When using paid or boosted media, ensure transparency in partnerships and consider various options like story ads, sponsored hashtags, and custom AR filters. Establish benchmarks for metrics, focusing on customer actions and business goals rather than just impressions.

Showcasing your brand personality with social media stories

In conclusion, we've covered the significance of social media stories in building awareness, expressing brand personality, showcasing products, and engaging customers. We explored strategies for developing your social story strategy, finding ideas, creating storyboards, assembling a team, adapting workflows, and enhancing stories. We've provided guidance on marketing social stories and measuring success. Now it's your turn to plan, produce, and promote stories that resonate with your audience.

www.ingramcontent.com/pod-product-compliance
Lightning Source LLC
Chambersburg PA
CBHW062302290526
45794CB00006B/2670